Written By Mary Mahone

It's Going To Be Okay copyright ©
2023 by Mary Mahoney

All rights reserved. This book or any portion
therof may not be reproduced or used in any
matter whatsoever without the expressed written
premission of the publisher except for the use
of brief quotations in a book review or social media post

Published by Mary Mahoney

P.O Box 821542 Vancouver, WA 98682

2023
979-8-218-95113-9

Introduction

At first this book was going to be titled "It's Going To Be Okay" and then I realized that sometimes things just aren't okay; And the reality is most of the time we feel like our feelings aren't okay. Every single one of the poems in this book were once written and quite literally were thrown in the trash; Because I thought they weren't okay.

Which had me thinking in the 8th grade my health teacher took a piece of printer paper in her hand and crumpled it up and she said "these are your mistakes" then she proceeded to open up the paper pointed to all the new folds, lines and creases and said "these are the scars your mistakes left you with, and after so many mistakes you wont be any good to nobody."

and tossed it in the trash.

I finally know what she meant

— Trash has character.
(if you think about it people turn trash to art every single day)

it's going to be okay

it's going to be okay one day
one day it's going to be okay
and the skies wont look so gray

— MM

Stuck

Same flaws different walls
still trying to figure out the cause
is it something i did wrong

— M.M.

i'm just trying to take it one day at a time
and it's slowly making me lose my mind

— M.M.

part 1

you'll text me and tell me that you're sorry

and ill say okay and hit send
when I really just want things between us to end
because how can you be my lover if you dont even feel like a friend

— M.M.

part 2

i learned that i am really good at playing pretend

nobody ever gets the same me over and over again

— M.M.

Exiting

you dont deserve to chase a love
that doesn't exist you deserve
the type of love
where you're missed before
you even reach the exit.

— M.M.

I hope you have time
for all you want to do
and i hope
the rest of world
doesn't give up on you
— M.M.

Wish You Meant Them

the hugs are nice but I wish you made me feel like i deserve them

the hugs are nice but I wish you were hugging me just to hold me close and not just because you feel bad for hurting me

the hugs are nice but I wish you didn't just make me cry so hard

the hugs are nice but i wish you actually meant them

— M.M.

Forgotten Self-Love

it's so hard to love yourself
when you're not being loved correctly
you really believe that how they're treating
 you is what you deserve

— even from yourself

Desire & Drive

I'm going to remember these long drives
Taking in everything as it transpires in front of me

Everything inspires me
On these long drives
I come up with new sentences to memorize

Oh, the things I desire

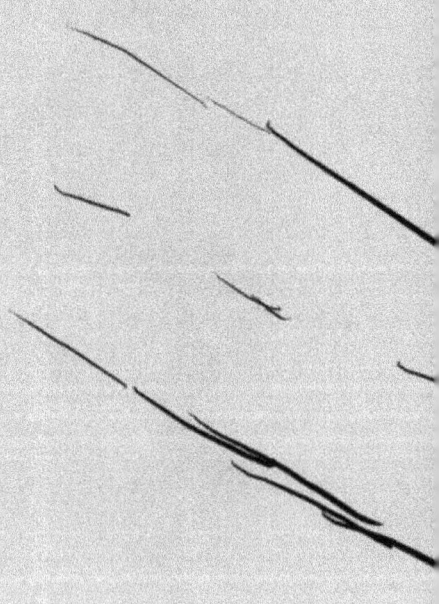

Unstable

I'm the emotially unstable,
the crazy one,
 I'm everything I used to let you call me
because of all the times
I wasn't me enough to stick up for myself

because i wanted to be where i didn't belong
and now though I'm not alone
I still feel alone

— M.M.

Time

I almost feel like the fact that time
 keeps moving is the part of life that scares me the most.

We don't get to sit in dwell in the good moments
no matter how bad we want to, time is always moving

— M.M. .

Just like a seed you grew

And when you grew so did I
no longer do I feel the need to hide

There is no longer that empty feeling
I have felt it inside for so long

I have purpose and
because of you I finally feel worth it

— M.M.

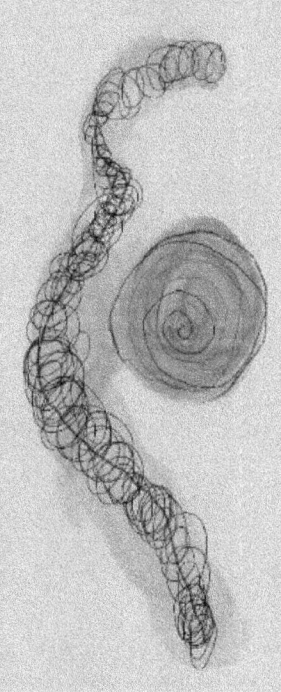

how is it fair for you to judge me for my past;

knowing that you have one too
and never
not once
have you thought about
putting yourself
in my shoes

— M.M.

i hate when i drink like this
but i pay attention to what
i cry about on nights like this

— M.M.

i love you to the liquor store and back

26

i had to live so many lives
before i knew this is the one
i wanted to live

and i know i'm only 26

but this is really it

— M.M.

things are starting to feel a little strange

like asking for rain on a sunny day

— M.M.

A Storm

people will flood your life
with negativity like a storm
that pours into your mind

but the sun eventually shines again
as clinche as it may sound

— M.M.

Sometimes we just expect the things that
we just don't deserve

But do we ever think about how that hurts
Do we think about how it would feel to have your jaw against a curb?

How bad does it hurt when expressing your feelings turns into something as pointless and a blurb on the back of a book

Knowing that you were never once heard.

Sometimes it's smart to keep your feelings reserved;
That it almost looks like you couldn't have a care in the world.

- M.M

Unfortunately

theres a lot of people
who are going to miss out
on a lot of things in life
because their teen years never ended.

— M.M.

Believe me,

I know I never deserved it

But imagine this,
being so used to it and so hurt by it
to the point that you actually
believe that you deserve it

At one point I let someone say they "love"
me but not understand what my worth is
How was I supposed to know that I was worth it?

I'll never again let another make me
feel so clueless.

— M.M

hopeless

when i feel hopeless i drink
when im drunk
i feel confident

confident that you still love me

— M.M.,

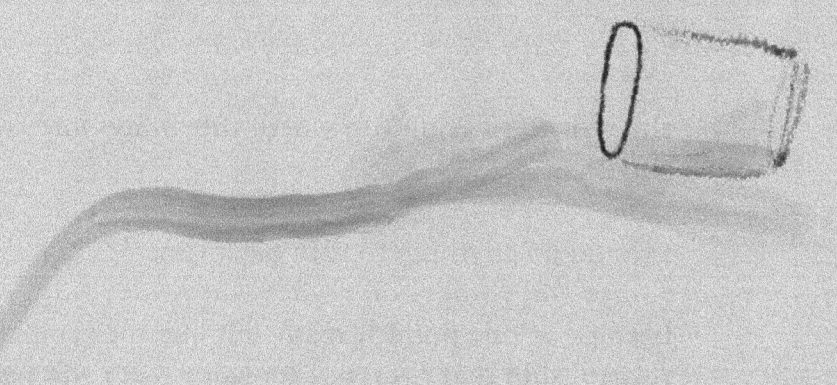

the type of relationship where you always lose track
the time,

i would do anything to turn back time

because at one point it really felt like the type of
relationship that everyone looks for but can't seem t
find

where you already know what the other is going to s
because you can practically read each other's minds

— M.M.

letting go and just trusting
that things were going to be okay
was the bravest thing
i've ever chose to do

stop

stop letting people
who don't share the same idea
of happiness as you
dictate your happiness

— M.M.

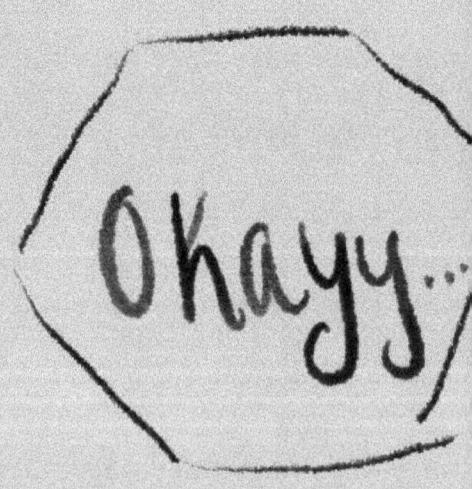

Sideways Elephant

i used to think you were heaven sent
but now nothing makes sense like a sideways elephant

— M.M.

narcissistic

and one day i hope you feel the slightest bit bad for all the times that you made me cry but you wont

— M.M.

Regrets

dating someone at the lowest point of your life can
either be the biggest blessing or the biggest curse

i want you to love me at my worst
but dont want you to only know me for my worst

at some point though
someone will be resilient enough
to see the good

they will love me

— M.M.

age is nothing but a number..

but it sucks that, the fact that i am so much
younger than you that these moments feel li[ke]
everything to me, and feel like nothing to yo[u]

- right

sometimes it's not what a relationship that shows you what love is sometimes it genuinely is your friends

maybe it's your family

maybe you're lucky enough
to have a chosen family

— M.M.

one day

one day im going to married to the man
who helped me heal the heart
that everyone else just
tore a little more

- one day

here's to the last kids to play outside with their friends the kids who realized life wasn't just a dead end job, the kids who realize what is being robbed from us in this lifetime. here's to the kids breaking generational trauma. here's to the kids taking care of their mamas; here's to the kids who are mamas. Here's to the kids who are stepping up and demanding mental health days because they forever changed the workplace. Here's to the kids that taught the world the importance of boundaries and personal space. Here's to the kids that know that there is a time and place. Here's to the kids that changed the world as a whole. Here's to the kids who still feel like they have

philanthropist
of my own life
— M.M.

how can i be your sunshine
if you wont stop the rain

how can you expect to
be my sunny day

if you won't stop blocking
the sun

— M.M.

To Do

I don't my life to become
A bunch of things I regret not doing
A list of things i wish i did

— M.M.

Unheard

i physically see you looking at me
but i know you dont see me

you're the definition of
what goes in one ear
goes out the other

— M.M.

i cannot continue to pretend that we want the same things i simply cannot continue to play a role in a play that was not written for me

— *M.M.*

not a friend

you could really build up a person; teach them things, help them grow

they'll grow until they are strong enough

strong enough to destroy you

— M.M.

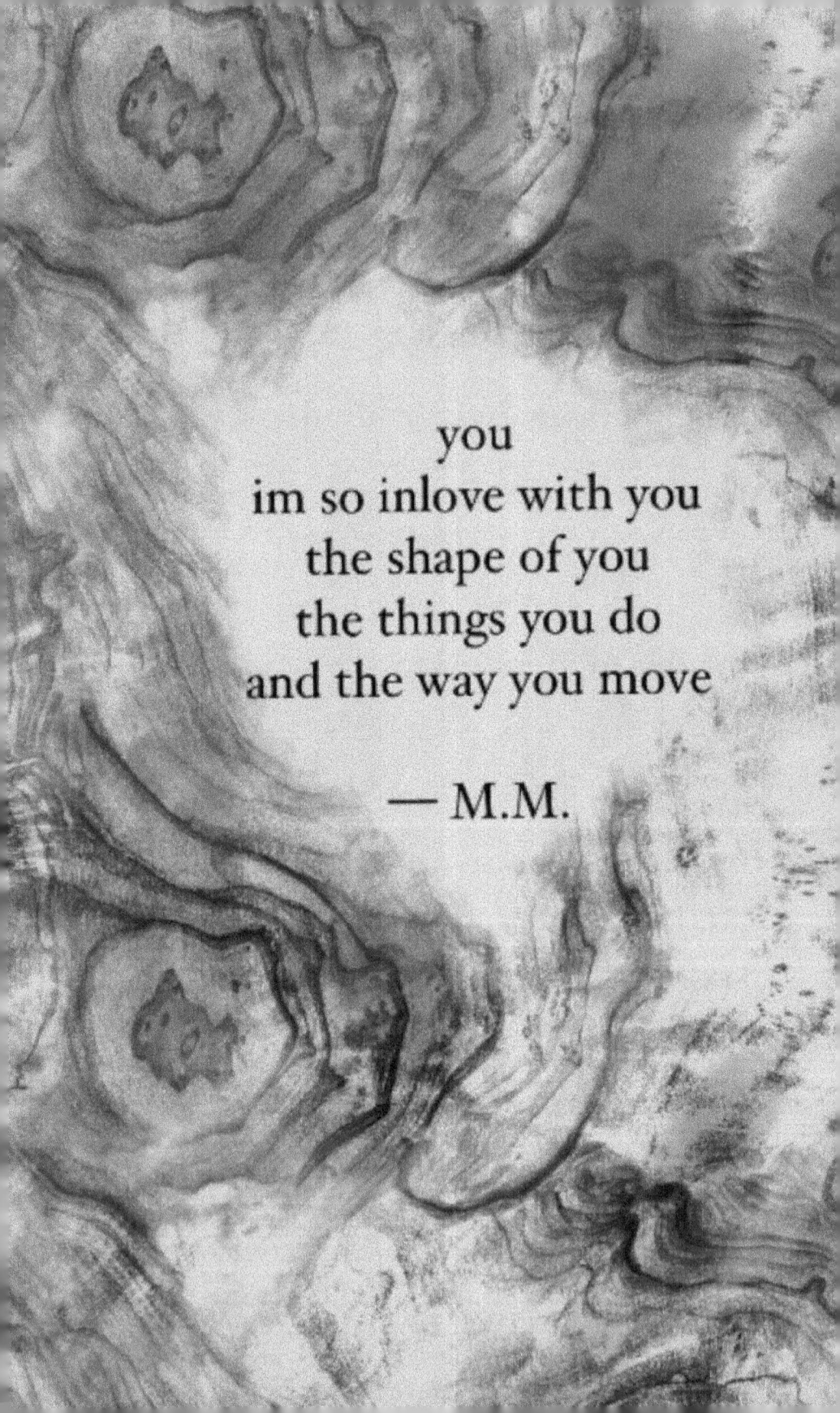

you
im so inlove with you
the shape of you
the things you do
and the way you move

— M.M.

sad GIRL

Im a sad girl
in a cruel word
this is drastic
im about to panic

you listen if you care

— M.M.

I can't believe there was a time that I loved you
more than myself
to a point where I was no longer who i was
but now
I'm a -

strong girl
sad girl
lonely girl

RESILIENT GIRL

my crown fell too many times and now theres not a crown to fix anymore. but I'll find a new one.

—Just as I alway do

different worlds

I hope in every alternative reality our paths cr

but don't cross in a way that they do in this or

I hope this is just the one off reality,
where you forgot to love me

— M.M.

The man that makes you leave home..

*Is supposed to give you so much love;
That it always feels like home*

— *M.M.*

Happy Home

Ive never thought about roots
or where i'd start my own

I just know I want it to start with a happy home

— M.M.

wants & needs

I want to raise kids
that won't need therapist

I need to see one first

— M.M.

understanding

you see if you knew how many time I told someone what would make me happy only for them to do the exact opposite, than maybe you would understand

— sometimes, I feel like I don't deserve to be happy

protect your mind not your heart
your heart can be ripped a part many times,
your mind cannot

— M.M.

baby steps

take the steps that no one expects
you to know to take
and follow your own pace

— M.M.

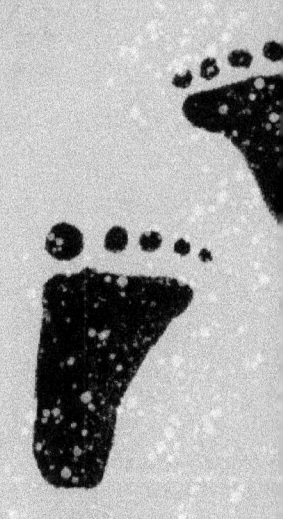

to think that i once
 thought it wasn't possible
to live this life

— everything works out for me

healing is really when you, and why

then you go take that mf back

— the power is ALWAYS yours

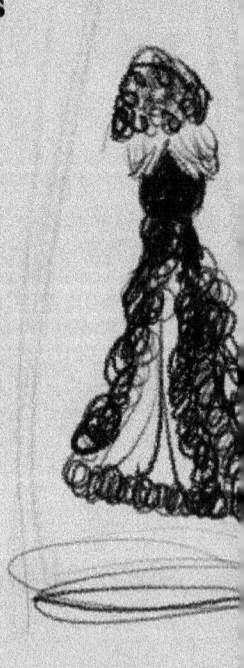

Sometimes I don't know if my art makes me want to cringe or cry

open arms

it would be nice to have someone love on after a long day, someone that is waiting for me with open arms after a long day and not a battle where were up in arms and lying about it causing no harm

- everyones harmed

life doesnt work out
the way you plan it to

because life wasn't meant
to be lived by a plan

- we've been fooled

Hold on..

I hate that I just want to fall in to your open arms

With no regard of the world around me
Not thinking about the pain you caused me
Because in your eyes things seem so good

But all I see in my eyes are things that sound good
and two people who are both so misunderstood

— M.M.

What A Woman Wants

I want to be the woman a man wants.
Not the bitch he puts up with

Didn't Ask

i promise i never asked
to be so fucked up
so cynical and stuck

imagine having the best of luck
with still no luck

— M.M.

DIY

I've spent a decade creating my own problems
and fixing them

A different type of creative if you will.
My own version of an artist

— M.M.

The voices in my head taught me
that there's a lot of things;
that can be left unsaid

I learned to keep a lot of shit in my hea[d]
and write
And it's okay for words to be left unrea[d]
If you tell me a secret
I'm taking it to my death bed

— M.M

Symphony

How do you let everything
that nigga say
stay in your head rent free?

That shit don't even sound
cool to me
like you really think
his game that smooth
like a symphony

— M.M.

i wish i could hear you think and i wish you would hear me speak

— M.M.

Questions

How do you know that situation
Is for you when it constantly
Gets flipped on you
80% of the time you
don't know what to do
And nobody feels bad for you

Cause this is really you;
Nothing is brand new
Like is it really that hard to
get this shit through to you

You like to play pretend
Like you'll end up with one
Of these niggas in the end.

— M.M.

It's not okay that you
can't stop hurting yourself
by letting others hurt you

-- M.M

Disregard

Disregard everything I've said
I don't know why I love so hard

— M.M

Shhh

heart breaks
fine wine

stop telling me,
that things get better with time

— M.M.

Stupid

I'm really writing this in my exes bed
While he's in another bitches bed

I don't think any else needs to be said

— M.M

it's a _____

in your twenties you date a lot of the type of men
you thought you would never even meet

the type of men that make your skin crawl;
 that send shivers up your spine.
 But then there will be the men,
the men that make you take everything in

but then you'll realize that this was never a two way street,
you'll finally walk out the door
 and now you're left feeling less complete than you were before.

— a cycle

Do You Ever

Do you ever get shivers,
Shivers from trying to think
about the things... the things
that you don't remember?

I kinda remember this one September,
Where everything felt a little better

The weight on my shoulders
Wasn't as heavy as it is now

But I can't remember what it was that
made it heavier

— M.M.

Favoritism

your favorite thing is your favorite thing
til it's no longer your favorite thing

'And your favorite person is only
your favorite person
 until they aren't anymore

— M.M.

www.ingramcontent.com/pod-product-compliance
Lightning Source LLC
Chambersburg PA
CBHW071411160426
42813CB00085B/1075